A Primary Source History of the Lost Colony of
ROANOKE

BRIAN BELVAL

rosen central
Primary Source™
The Rosen Publishing Group, Inc., New York

To Natalie

Published in 2006 by The Rosen Publishing Group, Inc.
29 East 21st Street, New York, NY 10010

Copyright © 2006 by The Rosen Publishing Group, Inc.

First Edition

Library of Congress Cataloging-in-Publication Data

Belval, Brian.
  A primary source history of the Lost Colony of Roanoke / Brian Belval.—1st ed.
      p. cm.—(Primary sources of the thirteen colonies and the Lost Colony)
  Includes bibliographical references and index.
  ISBN 1-4042-0435-0 (lib. bdg.)
  ISBN 1-4042-0669-8 (pbk. bdg.)
  1. Roanoke Colony—Juvenile literature. 2. Roanoke Island (N.C.)—History—16th century—Juvenile literature. 3. Roanoke Colony—Sources—Juvenile literature. 4. Roanoke Island (N.C.)—History—16th century—Sources—Juvenile literature.
  I. Title. II. Series.
  F229.B45 2006
  975.6'175–dc22

                                                                                                              2005001389

Manufactured in the United States of America

On the front cover: John White is seen with his group in this nineteenth-century illustration pointing to the inscription of the word CROATOAN, a clue presumably left by residents of his Roanoke colony. At the request of Roanoke's colonists, White had left the settlement to return to England for supplies but was unable to immediately return due to England's war with Spain.

CONTENTS

INTRODUCTION

The Mystery of Roanoke

In 1587, English colonists arrived at Roanoke, an island off the coast of present-day North Carolina. Shortly after their arrival, they worried about their ability to survive. They asked their governor, John White, to go back to England for supplies. White reached England safely, but his return trip to America was delayed after war broke out between England and Spain.

Three years later, White finally returned to Roanoke. When he reached the settlement, he discovered that all of the colonists had disappeared. Their homes were also gone—not a single board remained. The only clue that White found was the word "*CROATOAN*" carved into a fence post. He believed this meant that the colonists had moved to a nearby island. Unfortunately, White never made it there. A violent storm blew his ship off course, and the ship's captain refused to continue the search. White sailed back to England unsure of the fate of the 116 colonists. In the following decades, search parties sought them out, but never found them. To this day, their fate remains a mystery.

Many theories exist concerning the missing colonists. Some people believe that they were killed by Native Americans. Still others believe they attempted to sail back to England but were lost at sea. The most promising of these theories are supported, at least in part, by primary sources such as books, letters, drawings, and paintings that were written or made by people who had witnessed the events they described. These sources tend to be more accurate than sources gathered years later. Because of

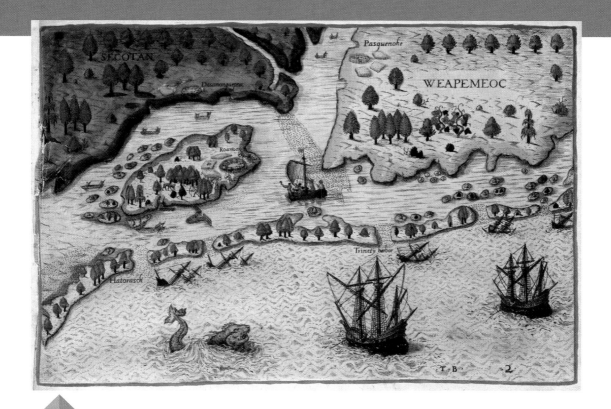

A drawing by John White, one of the original colonists in the ill-fated Roanoke expedition of 1585, was the foundation for this sixteenth-century engraving by Theodor de Bry called *The Arrival of the Englishmen in Virginia*. Published in England in 1590, de Bry's engraving showed the sinking of several British ships off the coast of what is now North Carolina, as well as the presence of a mythical sea creature in the Atlantic Ocean. The Roanoke colony (seen here as "Roanoac") is pictured, as are the names of several established Native American villages including Secotan, Weapemeoc, Pasquenoke, and Dasamonquepeuc.

this, historians rely highly on information drawn from primary sources in order to more accurately understand history.

A number of primary sources concerning Roanoke remain. Some of these items are featured throughout this book, giving you the chance to examine them just as a historian would.

CHAPTER 1

In 1492, the Italian explorer Christopher Columbus sailed across the Atlantic Ocean hoping to reach Asia. Instead, he discovered America and claimed it for the king of Spain. Over the next fifty years, Spanish men seeking wealth descended upon America. These men were known as conquistadors, or conquerors. The gold and silver they seized from native populations would make Spain the wealthiest, most powerful kingdom in the world.

While Spain gained wealth from its exploration of the New World, England watched from the outside. At the time, England was a kingdom in turmoil. Its king, Henry VIII, had broken relations with the Roman Catholic Church and declared himself the leader

England Challenges Spain

of a new church he named the Church of England. This caused great turmoil in English society. Many English citizens with ties to the Catholic Church lost their land and homes. These changes led to rebellion, especially in northern England. To make matters worse, England was at war with France and Scotland throughout Henry's reign. These conflicts depleted England's resources, so instead of funding expeditions to America, England was forced to solve its problems at home.

The situation in England worsened after Henry VIII died. Edward, Henry's only son, became king at age ten. Edward was sickly and died after only six years on the throne. Because of his youth and poor health, he was unable to provide the leadership England needed. Then, Henry's daughter Mary became queen. Mary was a Catholic and felt it was her duty to reestablish

Social and religious reform took shape in England under King Henry VIII (1491–1547), who reigned from 1509 until his death. Pictured (*left*) in an oil portrait by Hans Holbein the Younger, the court painter, King Henry provided solid leadership for England and helped bolster its defense, especially its naval fleet. Despite the king's hopes that his young son would rule after his death, Edward was too sickly and died of tuberculosis in 1553. Taking over for Edward was Henry's daughter, Mary Tudor, though her reign would end with her death in 1558. After, the throne was passed to Mary's half sister Elizabeth (1558–1603, *right*). Despite inheriting a dwindling treasury and a society disunited by religious differences, Queen Elizabeth's forty-four–year legacy was regarded as successful, especially considering her decisions to send expeditions to the New World.

England as a Catholic country. One of her methods to accomplish this goal was to execute people who opposed Catholicism. By the end of her reign, she was known as "Bloody Mary."

To undo the fear and distrust created during Mary's reign, England needed a strong, intelligent, and persuasive leader. Such a person was Queen Elizabeth I, the daughter of Henry VIII and

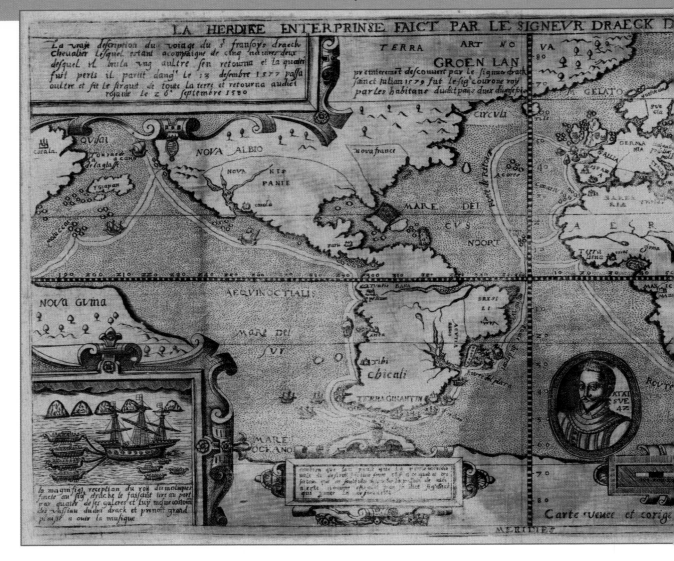

half sister of Mary. Elizabeth was crowned in 1558. One of Elizabeth's first acts was to restore the Church of England. The country rallied around the church, taking pride in the Protestant faith. Then Elizabeth went about improving relations with Scotland and France, two longtime enemies of England. She also passed laws to help improve England's economy. Before long, England prospered and set its sights on America.

During Elizabeth's reign, great mariners of England emerged from a coastal area called Devonshire. Here, generations of

This world map shows the route taken by the English navigator Sir Francis Drake who was knighted by Queen Elizabeth shortly after he returned from his voyage around the world in 1580. Drake returned to England with a tremendous quantity of gold, silver, jewels, and other precious items, which he bestowed upon the queen while recalling tales of his excursions to far-flung places. Because of Drake's success, England's wealth was restored and the country held claims to lands in the New World. When Drake was knighted he was given a coat of arms that read, *Sic Parvis Magna*, Latin for "Greatness from Small Beginnings." Later, in 1588 with England at war with Spain, Drake helped to successfully defend his homeland from Spain's mighty armada.

shipbuilders, merchants, and sailors had established a profitable trade with northern Europe. By the 1560s, they were actively seeking opportunities to expand their trade elsewhere. They were fascinated by the New World, but it was off-limits to them. The king of Spain, Philip II, did not allow his colonies in the Americas to trade with any country except Spain.

John Hawkins was the first of the men from Devonshire to challenge King Philip II. In 1562, Hawkins sailed to the New World with hundreds of African slaves he intended to sell to colonists. He knew his actions were illegal, but the colonists were willing to ignore the law because they desperately needed slaves to work their plantations. In 1567, after two successful slave-trading voyages, Hawkins returned for a third. This time the king was waiting for him. Philip had learned of the illegal trading and sent his warships to attack Hawkins. The warships intercepted Hawkins's fleet near Veracruz, Mexico. Hawkins lost four ships in the ensuing battle, and barely escaped with his life.

An English sailor named Francis Drake fought alongside Hawkins on that fateful day. Enraged by the aggression of the king of Spain, he sought revenge. By 1572, Drake was attacking Spanish ports in Central America and stuffing his vessels full of stolen treasure. Over the next decade, Drake would become the first Englishman to circumnavigate the globe. He returned to England a national hero and was knighted by Queen Elizabeth aboard his ship the *Golden Hind*.

Soon, English sailors had learned the easiest way to get rich was to steal from the Spanish. The Englishmen who challenged Spain in this way became known as "sea dogs," named after a type of shark common in English waters. Often these men received approval and even funds from the queen to rob Spanish ships. This activity was called privateering, and the men who took part in it were known as privateers.

In 1577, a sea dog named Sir Humphrey Gilbert submitted a proposal to the queen entitled *How Her Majesty May Annoy the King of Spain*. Part of Gilbert's plan was to seize Spanish fishing fleets in Newfoundland, a large island on the east coast of Canada. Although the queen disagreed with Gilbert's plan, she did give him permission to start a colony there. She felt, as did Gilbert and others, that the time had come for England to establish itself overseas.

Unfortunately, Gilbert failed. His first attempt to reach the New World in 1578 was disastrous and his ships returned to England. In 1583, Gilbert tried again. He made it to Newfoundland, but problems mounted after his arrival. Some of his men fled, hoping to hitch a ride back home on one of the ships in the harbor. Others decided to hijack a fishing vessel. Then, on a scouting mission off the coast, one of Gilbert's boats sank and their supplies were ruined. After less than a month in Newfoundland, Gilbert abandoned hope of starting a colony. The final disaster occurred on his return voyage when his ship capsized in a storm and he was drowned.

Luckily for England, its desire to settle the New World did not end with Gilbert. The spirit of exploration was passed on to Gilbert's half brother, Sir Walter Raleigh.

CHAPTER 2

Scouting the New World

Sir Walter Raleigh would eventually become the driving force behind the Roanoke colony. Born in 1554 in Devonshire, England, his family was influential in business and politics. At fifteen years of age, Raleigh went to France to make his name as a soldier. He fought beside the Huguenots, Protestant allies of England who were battling Catholic forces for control of the country. When Raleigh returned from France, he attended law school but didn't take his studies seriously. Instead, he spent his time writing poetry and drinking in local taverns. In 1578, he captained a ship in his half brother's unsuccessful attempt to colonize America. Then, in 1580, Raleigh returned to military service. He went to Ireland, where the Irish were rebelling against their English landlords. Raleigh helped put down the rebellion, overseeing the execution of all 600 residents of the town of Smerwick.

Raleigh's service in Ireland attracted the attention of Queen Elizabeth, who was searching for courageous leaders. Soon he became a member of the queen's court. In this position as a courtier, his responsibility was to entertain and flatter the queen. Raleigh excelled as a courtier. His charm, wit, and skill as a poet delighted Queen Elizabeth. She rewarded him with permission to collect taxes from area merchants. By the time of Sir Humphrey Gilbert's death in 1583, Raleigh was wealthy, ambitious, and hungry for fame. It was no surprise, then, that Elizabeth chose to transfer the right of colonization in North America to Raleigh, whom she affectionately referred to as her "Water."

POTENTISSIMAE ELIZABETHAE ANGLIAE REGINAE ad Nobilissimum D.num D.num HENRICUM CAREY, Baron de HUNSDON, Consobrinum suum in Villa de Hunsdon PROCESSIO REGALIS.

The Royal PROCESSION of QUEEN ELIZABETH to Visit the Right Hon.ble HENRY CAREY Lord HUNSDON, Governor of Berwick upon Tweed, Captain of the Band of Gentlemen Pensioners K. of the most Noble Order of the Garter, Privy Counceller and Cousin German to her Majesty by the Lady MARY, Sister to QUEEN ANNA BOLEN.

About 1,000 people made up the court of Queen Elizabeth I at any given time during her reign. Her every need was tended to and she was well guarded from potential adversaries. Even in Elizabeth's private moments, more than six maids could be found in her presence. Of her courtiers, among them Sir Walter Raleigh, the queen expected great intelligence and wit. In this eighteenth-century engraving, Raleigh is pictured among the court procession. Like other monarchs, Elizabeth moved from castle to castle throughout England (at the time of her accession she inherited sixty residences), and in this image she is being carried by armed guard to London.

Raleigh wasted no time putting together his expedition. A month after receiving permission from the queen, he had two ships outfitted to sail to the New World. His mission was to hire a crew to scout suitable locations in America for a colony. Ideally, his crew would locate an area with a harbor close to Spain's colonies, but also

John White (about 1557–1593), sixteenth-century English artist and governor of the 1587 colony, was responsible for some of our most exquisite and valuable paintings of Native American life in Virginia. This watercolor, *The Manner of Their Fishing*, was an invented scene, a combination of several studies of Native Americans and their fishing practices that were observed by White in the New World. According to his notes, the Algonquin used a dip net and spear for day fishing and a fire in a canoe to attract fish at night.

hidden from them. Twenty years earlier, the French had established Fort Caroline in Florida, but the Spanish had destroyed it.

Raleigh wanted the colony to serve as a base for privateering. In the past, privateers would sail across the Atlantic, meet Spanish ships, and then travel back to England. A colony closer to the Spanish treasure fleet would be much more convenient and profitable.

On April 27, 1584, Raleigh's two ships left England. Raleigh chose Philip Amadas to lead the expedition, while Arthur Barlowe captained the smaller vessel. On July 4, after more than two months at sea, they spotted land and claimed it for England.

Initially the men thought they had landed on the North American mainland. However, they soon realized they were on an island about 20 miles (32 kilometers) long and 6 miles (10 km) wide. (Today we know this island as one in the chain off the coast of North Carolina called the Outer Banks. The exact island where they landed is still debated, but it was likely Hatarask Island.) As they explored, the Englishmen found woods full of deer, rabbits, and birds. In the words of Barlowe, the island was teeming with animals "in incredible abundance."

On the third day, a lone Native American appeared on the beach directly across from the Englishmen's ships. A group of Englishmen, including Amadas and Barlowe, rode out to meet him. The Indian delivered a speech to the men, not a word of which they understood. The Englishmen brought the Native American to their ship, where he was given a shirt and a hat. They also offered him wine and meat.

After he was given a tour of both ships, the Native American returned to the shore. He immediately sought out his boat and began fishing. Within thirty minutes he had packed his boat full of fish. On the shore, he neatly divided his catch into two piles. The

Native American pointed at each pile and then to each anchored ship. The fish were gifts in return for the Englishmen's gifts.

In the days that followed, the English traded extensively with the Native Americans, exchanging some of their less valuable items for animal skins, leather, dyes, and coral. The Native Americans also expressed great interest in the Englishmen's metal swords, which were superior to their own wooden ones. But the English refused to trade their swords, fearing they might be used against them.

Throughout this period, the Native Americans were generous. Every day Granganimeo, the brother of the Indian king Wingina, brought the explorers food—deer, rabbit, fish, fruit, melons, walnuts, and an assortment of vegetables including corn. During this time they were also introduced to Granganimeo's wife, whom Barlowe described as being "bashful."

Although the Englishmen and the Native Americans spoke different languages, they were still able to communicate using gestures and sign language. The explorers learned that the king of the tribe was named Wingina and that he had been injured while fighting rival Native Americans. Because he was recuperating in a distant village, Amadas and Barlowe were unable to meet him.

Of course, occasional misunderstandings occurred between the two groups. For example, when the explorers asked one of the Native Americans the name of his country, he misunderstood them, and replied, "Wingandacoa," which meant, "You wear nice clothes." From then on, the explorers mistakenly referred to the country as Wingandacoa.

After establishing good relations with the Native Americans, Barlowe and seven other men decided it was safe to go scouting. Twenty miles (32 km) into their journey, they reached a Native American settlement on the north end of Roanoke Island. As they

This lithograph, a map of the North American coastline and Chesapeake Bay, is a copy of a painting by John White. It was created sometime between 1570 and 1593. Just off the coast of what is now North Carolina, in the mid-left section of the drawing (and in the detail, *inset*), sits Roanoke Island. It was then known as "Roanoac," a name attributed to the Indian king Roanoac, who may have lived there prior to the arrival of the Europeans. To the Algonquin, *Roanoac* may also have meant "northern people" or may have been a reference to shell beads.

approached, Granganimeo's wife rushed out to meet them, delighted by their surprise visit.

Granganimeo's wife treated the men well. She had them carried back to her village, which consisted of nine homes made out of cedar wood. The explorers were brought inside her home and seated in front of the fire. According to Barlowe, "She took off our clothes and washed them and dried them." Then, her attendants washed the explorers' feet.

The landing of the Englishmen at Roanoke Island is depicted in this nineteenth-century print. Although historians speculate as to when Englishmen first set foot in the New World (some claim as early as 1475), it is well documented that England's finest achievements in exploration came under the leadership of Queen Elizabeth beginning in 1558. Although colonization didn't occur until the late 1580s, many earlier English fishermen wintered in the New World during long expeditions.

After they were refreshed, Granganimeo's wife led the explorers into a room where a feast had been prepared. The men ate happily, enjoying the bounty.

Suddenly, the festive tone of the dinner was interrupted when Barlowe and his men caught sight of a group of Native Americans carrying bows and arrows. Even though they meant no harm, the sight of their weapons alarmed the group. Granganimeo's wife noticed that the Englishmen were uncomfortable. She asked her servants to confiscate the bows. Then, the

Sir Walter Raleigh (1554–1618) is pictured on the engraved title page of *The Historie of the World*, a chronicle of world events first published in 1614. Raleigh began writing his *Historie* while imprisoned in the Tower of London. He was first sent there by Queen Elizabeth after she discovered that he was secretly married to one of her maids, Elizabeth Throckmorton. Though he was soon released, he was again imprisoned in 1603 after James I read *Historie* and found him guilty of treason. Although he was released in 1616, he was executed two years later. See page 54 for an excerpt from *The Historie of the World*.

servants broke the bows to prove that they would not harm their guests.

Still, the Englishmen were worried. When they announced they had to leave, Granganimeo's wife begged them to stay. It did not matter that they'd witnessed the bows destroyed. They knew there were others, and they weren't willing to take any risks. Instead of sleeping in the village, they slept on their boat. When daylight arrived, they returned to the main ships.

By mid-August, the scout group left America for England. Two Native Americans named Manteo and Wanchese joined them. The

Englishmen hoped to teach English to the Native Americans so they could act as interpreters on future voyages.

Back in England, Barlowe prepared a report for Raleigh that said that Roanoke Island appeared to be ideal for a colony. Barlowe noted how it was situated at a safe distance from the Spanish colonies. Roanoke was also hidden from view of passing ships and would be difficult to find if one didn't know exactly where to look. Additionally, Roanoke and the surrounding islands had enough deer and fish to support a colony and its soil was believed to be good for farming. Perhaps most important, the Native Americans were friendly. As Barlowe put it, "We found the people most gentle, loving, and faithful."

CHAPTER 3

Even before Philip Amadas and Arthur Barlowe returned, Sir Walter Raleigh was busy preparing for the next voyage. The optimistic report he received from Barlowe accelerated his plans. He worked feverishly to find influential people to support his colony. To advertise the project, Manteo and Wanchese were introduced to potential investors, including Queen Elizabeth. Most of the people who met the Indians were impressed by them.

By April of 1585, Raleigh had a fleet ready to sail to Roanoke. His colony was to be named Virginia after Elizabeth, the "Virgin Queen." Elizabeth provided the flagship, the *Tiger*. She also provided an accomplished military leader, Ralph Lane, to act as governor of the colony. Raleigh, however, would not be joining the colonists in America. Elizabeth insisted that he was too valuable in England.

The Military Colony

Instead of Raleigh, Sir Richard Grenville was put in charge of the fleet. Grenville, Raleigh's cousin, had distinguished himself as a soldier in Ireland and as a sheriff in England. The lead pilot of the expedition was Simon Fernandez, who was also the pilot on the first voyage to Roanoke. He would be responsible for making sure they reached their destination safely.

On April 9, 1585, with Fernandez at the helm of the *Tiger*, the seven ships left England with 600 men. Their goal was to establish a base for raids against Spanish ships.

On June 22, the fleet arrived at the area now known as the Outer Banks. They sailed to Wococon Island, about 80 miles (129 km) south of Roanoke Island. Grenville and Lane had quarreled for much

Most historians believe this is a portrait of Thomas Harriot (1560–1621, *left*, also spelled Hariot), a friend and colleague of Sir Walter Raleigh's. At various periods, he served as Raleigh's accountant, ship designer, cartographer, and navigational instructor for his crews. In 1585, Harriot accompanied Raleigh's second expedition to Virginia under Sir Richard Grenville and acted as the group's historian. Harriot detailed his observations about the New World in *A Briefe and True Report of the New Found Land of Virginia*, which was first published in 1590. The title page is pictured on the right. See page 54 for a transcription.

of the journey. Each sent letters back to England claiming the other had failed to do his job. According to Lane, Grenville had become so furious that he threatened to execute him.

Then, tragedy nearly struck as Fernandez led the ships too close to land as the fleet approached Wococon. Ocean waves slammed the flagship into a shoal. Fernandez managed to save the ship, but many of their supplies got spoiled. Without these supplies, the colonists would have to find other ways to feed themselves.

While the *Tiger* was being repaired, fifty men in four separate boats traveled to the mainland. Over a week, they visited three Native American villages.

Joining Grenville on this expedition were two men who would become forever associated with the Roanoke colony—Thomas Harriot and John White. Harriot was a scientist, writer, and explorer. Raleigh asked him to join the expedition in order to provide a detailed study of the land and its people. Harriot, three years later, published his findings in *A Briefe and True Report of the New Found Land of Virginia*. In it, Harriot detailed all the American resources that might be of interest to English people. These included sassafras, tobacco, cedar wood, otter furs, iron and copper, pearls, turpentine, corn, oysters, and animal skins. Harriot wrote enthusiastically about both the abundance and the quality of these items. He referred to them as commodities, indicating that he believed they could be sold to English people or people in other countries.

In addition to describing New World resources, Harriot wrote about Native American culture and religion in his book. In one passage, he described how when the Englishmen kneeled to pray, the Indians kneeled and pretended to pray beside them. To the Englishmen, this suggested that the Native Americans were eager to convert to Christianity. In Harriot's words, the Native Americans were "poor souls" who were "very desirous to know the truth." That truth was "the knowledge of the gospel."

White was the colony's artist. His job was to draw the Native Americans, plants, and animals of Virginia. One of White's best drawings is of the village of Secota, which the Grenville party reached on July 15, 1585. Historians have gained an understanding

John White produced this famous drawing of the Indian village of Secota while in the company of Raleigh's 1585 expedition to Roanoke. Researching Native Americans around the Carolina coast, White observed this scene of everyday life. Later, around 1590, Theodor de Bry made engravings based on White's observational drawings, including this one. The de Bry engravings were then printed in Harriot's *A Briefe and True Report of the New Found Land of Virginia.*

of what a sixteenth-century Native American village looked like from his rendering.

The day after visiting Secota, the Englishmen discovered that a silver cup was missing. They determined that it was stolen during their visit to the village of Aquascogoc a few days earlier. Grenville instructed a group to return to the village and ask for the cup back. When the colonists didn't receive it, they burned down the village and its cornfields. The action was meant to discourage Indians from unlawful behavior. This harsh discipline was familiar to Lane, Grenville, and the other soldiers. England's military had been using similar tactics for years in Ireland and France.

After the colonists burned Aquascogoc, they returned to their ships. The *Tiger* had been repaired and they were ready to move north to Roanoke Island. They arrived at the harbor near Roanoke on July 29. Fernandez didn't risk running the boat ashore again. He anchored miles away from the island. By now it was becoming clear to Grenville and Lane that Roanoke and the adjacent islands may not be the best place for their colony. Because of the shallow water surrounding the islands, large ships like the *Tiger* had to stay miles offshore in deeper water. This meant that supplies had to be transferred to the island in small boats. In effect, Roanoke would be acceptable as a temporary colony, but eventually Amadas and Barlowe would need a location where larger ships could more easily make their approach.

Shortly after the ships reached the Roanoke harbor, Granganimeo rowed out to welcome them. The good relations established by Amadas and Barlowe had held, and Granganimeo gave the Englishmen permission to build their fort on Roanoke. Immediately, Grenville dispatched a ship back to England to report the good news.

Once they arrived on the island, the colonists set about building homes and a central fort for protection. By August, the fort was completed. Grenville left Roanoke for England, while 107 men, including Governor Lane, stayed behind. The plan was for Grenville to return with supplies the following spring. In the meantime, Lane's colony was supposed to explore the surrounding area for a more suitable site.

On September 3, Lane wrote a letter to Richard Hakluyt, an important promoter of English colonization. In the letter, Lane wrote about Virginia, "it is the goodliest and most pleasing territory of the world."

Still, one of the most important issues for the colonists was the depletion of food. Since most of their food had spoiled, they would need to find more. Growing crops was not an option because they had arrived too late in the season. Instead the colonists looked to the Native Americans for food. Initially this wasn't a problem. The Native Americans had a surplus of corn and were willing to share it.

By March of the next year, however, the relations between the Indians and the colonists had soured. Part of the problem was that Granganimeo, King Wingina's brother, had passed away. He was a good friend to the colonists and encouraged his people to cooperate with the Englishmen. King Wingina wasn't as friendly. He believed the colonists were a burden to his tribe. They were 107 extra men to feed, but did little to contribute to the health and safety of the community. In fact, as their attack on the village of Aquascogoc illustrated, they were capable of sudden acts of violence.

In March, Lane and a group of Englishmen left Roanoke Island to explore an area to the northwest known today as Albemarle Sound in search of a better location. But Lane was also interested

English writer Richard Hakluyt (1552–1616) was among England's strongest supporters of colonization in the New World. Besides important works including *The Principal Navigations*, in which he wrote about contemporary voyages to the New World, Hakluyt also wrote *Discourse of Western Planting* in 1584, a page of which is pictured here. The overwhelming arguments presented in *Discourse* suggest a variety of economic and political advantages that could be gained by England if the country would fund colonies in America. See the transcription on pages 55-56.

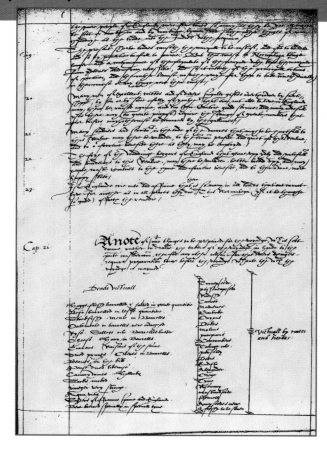

in finding treasure. He had heard of lands that produced copper and pearls in great amounts, and possibly even gold.

The men traveled 130 miles (209 km) to the village of Choanoke. There they met with Menatonon, the Choanoke king. Lane described him as "a man impotent [crippled] in his limbs, but otherwise for a Savage, a very grave and wise man." In order to learn where he could find pearls or gold, Lane and his men took Menatonon prisoner. He confirmed that there were two separate nations, one famous for its pearls, the other for "wassador," which was what the Indians called metal. This area known for its metal (probably copper) was called Chaunis Temoatan. Here, the precious metal was rumored to be so abundant that local tribes built their homes out of it.

While Lane held Menatonon captive, Menatonon confessed that Wingina was conspiring against the Englishmen by spreading rumors that the Englishmen were coming to wage war on Menatonon's tribe. Lane assured Menatonon that this was untrue. He accused Wingina of trying to strike fear into the Choanokes so that they would kill Lane and his men.

Before Lane left Choanoke, he wanted to make sure Menatonon was on his side. So he released Menatonon—and took his son prisoner instead. The son, Skiko, was sent off to Roanoke as a hostage.

The remaining group of thirty men took two boats up the Roanoke River in search of Chaunis Temoaton. They had packed very little food for the journey and hoped to get additional supplies from local Native Americans. However, all of the Native American villages had been deserted. Lane suspected that Wingina had warned the villagers of the Englishmen's approach. Without Indian corn, the Englishmen soon ran out of food. They were forced to turn back. On their return voyage, the situation became so desperate they had to make a stew out of their two guard dogs.

Back at Roanoke, the Englishmen eagerly waited for Sir Richard Grenville to arrive from England with fresh supplies. In the meantime, Lane continued to ask Wingina for food, but every time he was denied. The previous year's surplus of corn was depleted, and the Indians had nothing left to spare. Instead, Wingina planted a field of corn for the Englishmen. However, it would be two months before the corn was ready to harvest.

Lane's men foraged the neighboring islands for food. They survived by eating clams and wild game. These were hard times for the Englishmen. As they faced starvation, they probably blamed their woes on the Native Americans. Now the English and the Indians were enemies.

Richard Grenville (1542–1591) was an English naval officer who commanded the fleet of vessels carrying the first colonists to Virginia in 1585. Not long after his arrival, Grenville burned an Indian village, claiming that local tribes had stolen a silver cup. The burning of the village is re-created in this hand-colored woodcut.

Soon, a rumor reached Lane. Wingina was planning a surprise attack. The plan was to burn the fort and the surrounding homes and drive the Englishmen off the island. After weighing his options, Lane decided to act first. On the night of June 1, 1586, Lane and twenty-five men crossed Roanoke Sound to Wingina's village, Dasemunkepeuc. Pretending to want to meet with the king on friendly terms, the men were allowed to enter the village. Once inside, Lane shouted the signal to attack, "Christ Our Victory!" The Englishmen opened fire. A number of Indians were hit, including Wingina, who fell to the ground. Miraculously, Wingina got up and sprinted toward the woods. A number of English soldiers gave chase. A few minutes later, an English soldier emerged from the woods carrying Wingina's head.

While Lane attacked Wingina at Dasemunkepeuc, a fleet of thirty ships approached Roanoke. On June 8, one of Lane's soldiers spotted the English fleet. It was Sir Francis Drake and his band of privateers, returning from a successful raid against the Spanish. They had decided to stop by Roanoke on their way back to England.

On June 10, Lane met with Drake on his flagship. Drake understood the men were desperate. He offered Lane two choices. Drake could provide Lane with men, boats, and enough supplies for thirty days. This would allow him to continue his exploration of Virginia until Grenville arrived with more food. Or Lane and his men could return on Drake's ships back to England. Lane accepted the first offer. He wanted to forge ahead with his mission. Then, a fierce storm struck on June 13, sinking a number of ships in Drake's fleet. Most of the supplies were lost or ruined. Lane saw this as a sign that he was meant to return to England. In his words, "The very hand of God as it seemed, stretched out to take us from there." On June 19, the colonists boarded Drake's ships and set sail for England.

One month later, Sir Richard Grenville finally returned to Roanoke with supplies and reinforcements. When he found the colony deserted, he chose fifteen of his men to hold the fort, and returned to England.

CHAPTER 4

Sir Walter Raleigh must have been extremely disappointed when he learned that Ralph Lane had abandoned the colony. He had invested a considerable amount of his fortune in the colonization effort and had nothing to show for it. Still, his belief in England's destiny to colonize in America could not be shaken.

John White, the artist in Lane's colony, led the effort to organize the third colony, the City of Raleigh. White would also become its governor.

John White's Colony

The motivation behind this colony differed from that of the previous effort. Instead of a colony of soldiers, this would be a colony of families who personally invested in the venture. In return for their investment, they would receive a portion of any money made by the colony. Also, unlike the soldiers who were expected to stay at the colony for shifts of a few years, these colonists intended to stay in America permanently. To encourage this, each head of household would receive 500 acres (202 hectares) of land. They were expected to farm the land and be able to support themselves. Ideally, they would also develop products that could be sold for profit in Europe.

It was difficult for White to find people interested in resettlement. The majority of people were unwilling to live half way across the world in a land inhabited by "savages." In the end, White persuaded 116 colonists to come to America.

Everyone involved in the City of Raleigh agreed that it would have to be established somewhere other than Roanoke Island

John White made this fanciful watercolor painting of several hundred miles of what is now the eastern coast of the United States, including areas around the Chesapeake Bay and northern Florida. Instructed by Sir Walter Raleigh to "draw to life one of each kind of thing that is strange to us in England," White produced accurate and detailed images of plants, animals, fish, and portraits of many of the Native Americans showcasing their customs and dress. Little is known about White, who was ultimately a better artist than governor. Some historians believe that he also accompanied the English explorer Martin Frobisher on his voyage to the Arctic in 1577 prior to joining Raleigh's Roanoke expedition.

since it was unsuitable for ships to approach. Also, there was concern over how receptive the Roanoke Indians would be to another English colony in their territory. The fact that the previous English visitors had killed Wingina and became enemies of the Native Americans worried the new colonists. Would the Roanoke Indians be willing to live peacefully beside them?

The City of Raleigh was instead planned to be established near Chesapeake Bay. Some of Lane's men had visited this area and described it favorably. In the Chesapeake, the water was deeper and would accommodate larger ships. In addition, the bay was somewhat protected from unpredictable and violent weather.

Three ships were ready to leave England on May 8, 1587. Simon Fernandez piloted the flagship, the *Lion*. Of the 117 colonists, nine were children and two were pregnant women.

Eight days later, one of the vessels fell behind and lost contact with the fleet. White blamed Fernandez. He accused Fernandez of intentionally "leaving her [the ship] distressed in the Bay of Portugal." It was the first of many complaints White would have concerning Fernandez's behavior during the voyage.

The remaining ships reached the island of St. Croix on June 22. The colonists left the boats and explored the lush, tropical surroundings that looked nothing like England. Their curiosity, however, would soon get the best of them. According to White,

At our first landing on this island, some of our women, and men, by eating a small fruit, like green apples, were fearfully troubled with a sudden burning in their mouths, and swelling of their tongues so big, that some of them could not speak.

Later, some of the colonists washed their faces in a pond that turned out to be poisoned. The next morning, according to White's account, "their faces did so burn and swell that their eyes were shut up, and they could not see for five or six days or longer." This must have been a rude awakening for many of the colonists who now realized that danger was everywhere.

Pefe pica.

This image by John White is of one type of fish prevalent in the Northeast. White's drawings remain one of America's best sources of information about conditions in the New World in the late 1500s. White's detailed paintings and maps presented Europeans with the opportunity to view a firsthand account of life on another continent. The images he created of Native Americans, their customs, and the animals of the region helped to inspire Europeans to colonize America in the years that followed.

By July 16, the two ships reached Virginia. White then accused Fernandez of being careless and ignorant after he almost wrecked the *Lion*. Six days later, the colonists arrived at the harbor near Roanoke Island. They had received instructions from Raleigh to check on the men left behind by Grenville, then to continue north to Chesapeake Bay to establish the new colony.

White and forty men boarded the smaller boat called a pinnace in order to reach Roanoke. As they prepared to leave, Fernandez shouted at the crewmen on the boat to not return the colonists to the *Lion*. He intended to take them no farther than Roanoke. According to Fernandez, "The summer was far spent." By this, he meant that he had wasted too much time away from what he really wanted to do—privateering. Fernandez wanted to get rid of the colonists so that he could sail off and steal treasure from the Spanish.

Surely, this must have been a great shock to White, but he was powerless to fight back. Fernandez was the pilot of the ship, and his crew was behind him. If they were determined to leave the colonists at Roanoke, then they could not be stopped.

A greater shock awaited White and his men during their search for the fifteen men left behind by Grenville. White wrote in his journal, "We found none of them, nor any sign that they had been there, saving only we found the bones of one of those fifteen, which the Savages had slain long before."

Despite this grisly discovery, White ordered the colonists to repair the abandoned homes. He also ordered the construction of additional homes to accommodate the colonists. White was attempting to make the best of a bad situation.

Good news finally arrived on July 25 when the vessel that had been abandoned by Fernandez in the Bay of Portugal arrived at Roanoke. Miraculously, its pilot, Edward Spicer, was able to locate Virginia even though he had never been there before. According to White, this was "a great joy and comfort of the whole company." Now all 116 colonists had arrived at the island. Although they were surely disappointed to be dropped off short of their destination, at least they had the comfort of knowing the entire company had arrived safely.

For the first few days on the island, the colonists did not encounter any Native Americans. This may have given the colonists a false sense of security. Soon, however, their vulnerability would be exposed. One of the colonists, George Howe, wandered away. He was wading in shallow water, hunting crabs, when a group of Native Americans attacked. According to White, "they gave him sixteen wounds with their arrows, and after they had slain him with their wooden swords, beat his head in pieces."

After this incident, a group of colonists traveled to a nearby island called Croatoan, which was home to Manteo, the Englishmen's interpreter. Since Manteo was now living with the Englishmen, they hoped the Croatoans would be friendly. In White's words, he was hoping the Native Americans would "accept our friendship . . . and that all unfriendly dealings past on both parties, should be utterly forgiven and forgotten." The Croatoans agreed to gather leaders from the local villages and bring them to Roanoke to discuss the Englishmen's offer of peace.

The Croatoans also revealed to the Englishmen the fate of the fifteen colonists left behind by Grenville. Wingina's tribe ambushed the men shortly after they arrived. One of them was killed immediately, while the others retreated to the fort. The Indians forced the Englishmen out of the fort by setting it on fire. The two groups fought outside of the fort where another Englishman was killed. Then the remaining colonists fled to the water. They rushed into their boat and sailed away, never to be seen again. No one knows if they attempted to return to England, or if they searched for a new place to settle. Either way, they probably died shortly thereafter.

After meeting with the Croatoans, the Englishmen returned to Roanoke. There they waited for the arrival of the Indian leaders for seven days. After the week had passed, the Englishmen interpreted the lack of response as a rejection of their offer

Based on direct observations made by John White in the 1580s, Englishman Theodor de Bry created a series of hand-colored engravings for Thomas Harriot's *A Briefe and True Report of the New Found Land of Virginia* (1590). Among them is the one seen here, called *A Great Lord of Virginia*.

of peace. White then decided to attack the Native Americans at Dasemunkepeuc to avenge the murder of George Howe.

The Englishmen arrived at Dasemunkepeuc on the morning of August 9 and silently approached the village. When they saw a group of Native Americans around an open fire, they attacked without warning. The soldiers shot one of the Indians and pursued the others into the woods. Soon, they realized the Indians were not Wingina's men but Croatoans. They had attacked the only Indians who had remained friendly to them! The Croatoans explained that Wingina's men had fled Dasemunkepeuc soon after Howe's death. They had anticipated the Englishmen would come after them, and had moved deep into their territory for protection. The Croatoans were there to gather the corn left behind by the Roanoke settlers when they fled.

White reported that Manteo grieved over the unfortunate attack on his people, but at the same time blamed them for their misfortune. He told his people that if they would have brought the Indian leaders to Roanoke as promised, the attack would not have happened. It's unclear how the Croatoans felt about Manteo's statements, but most likely they felt betrayed by him.

A few days after the attack, the colonists rewarded Manteo for his loyalty to England. White appointed him as lord of Dasemunkepeuc. The title gave him control of the land previously ruled by Wingina. He was also baptized, making him the first Native American to convert to the Church of England.

On August 18, another landmark event occurred. Eleanor Dare, the daughter of John White, gave birth. Her daughter, Virginia Dare, became the first English person born in America. It must have been a joyous day for White and the colonists. They celebrated the birth of a healthy, beautiful child, and for that day were able to put aside their fears.

But other matters soon surfaced. The colony decided that at least one of the colonists should return to England for supplies. Well aware of the difficulty Lane's colony had in receiving fresh supplies, they wanted a representative at home to ensure that the shipments were sent in a timely manner. Because they had alienated all the local tribes, the grave danger of not receiving food became increasingly obvious to them.

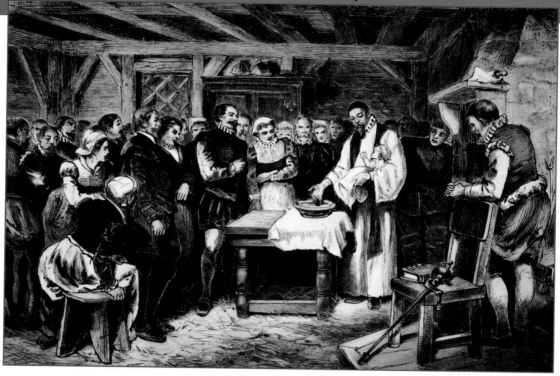

This nineteenth-century image represents one artist's conception of the historical baptism of Virginia Dare, the first baby born to Europeans in the New World. She was born in August 1587 to Eleanor Dare, daughter of John White, and Ananias Dare. Tragically, White never got to know his granddaughter since she disappeared along with all of the Roanoke colonists between 1587 and 1588. White left Roanoke to obtain supplies, but was delayed in England due to the country's war with Spain.

The men came to White and asked him to return to England. At first, he refused. He didn't think it was right for the leader of the colony to abandon it. They still hadn't decided where they should move the colony. White wanted to influence that decision and he feared that he would be judged unfairly in England if he returned and left the colonists behind. Would he look like a coward? In addition, if he returned to England, he wouldn't be there for his daughter and grandchild.

But the colonists returned the next day and asked again. They put their request in writing and signed it. This was important to White, because now he could present this letter to anyone in England who questioned why he would leave his colony behind. Despite his reservations, and the sadness that he must have felt about leaving his daughter and granddaughter behind, White agreed to leave the colony on August 27.

CHAPTER 5

J ohn White nearly didn't make it back to England. Three weeks into his journey, a powerful storm blew his ship back toward America. It took him seven days to return to the spot where he had been struck by the storm. Then his crew became ill and two men died. To make matters worse, their drinking water had become desperately low. White estimated that they had only three gallons (eleven liters) of liquids—beer, wine, and water—to be shared by thirteen men. White wrote in his journal, "We expected nothing but by famine to perish at sea."

The Lost Colony

Remarkably, on October 16, 1587, the men, weak, thirsty, and starving, spotted land. They were lost, however, and not until a boat came out to greet them did they know their location. They had reached Smerwick, in western Ireland. Many of the men remained sick, and shortly after their arrival three more died.

White fared better than his crew. He was well enough to take the first ship out to England. He reached Cornwall, the westernmost county of England, on November 5.

White met with Sir Walter Raleigh. He described the colony's situation and asked for help. Raleigh remained supportive of the colony. He decided to send a small ship immediately with a portion of the needed supplies. Then, he would send a larger relief fleet in the spring of 1588.

Soon it became clear that no ships would set sail for Roanoke in 1587. The Spanish Armada was preparing to attack England to avenge years of raids by English privateers. The king of Spain's plan was to strike back at England with one of the largest fleets

Hendrik Cornelisz Vroom painted this image in oil of a sea battle between the Spanish Armada and the English navy in 1600. The invasion of the Spanish Armada on English shores in 1588 was an attempt by King Phillip of Spain to overthrow England and restore the power of the Catholic Church. Although its navy was greatly outnumbered by the immense Spanish fleet, a combination of trickery and bad weather foiled the Spaniards' attempt to take over the country.

ever assembled. In response, Queen Elizabeth recalled all of England's ships to help defend the country.

Despite this setback, White didn't give up. After much effort, he was given permission to use two smaller ships. Because of their size and poor condition, they would be of no use in the defense against Spain, but acceptable for White's purpose.

The *Brave* and the *Roe* left England on April 22, 1588. They carried supplies and eleven colonists recruited by White. It soon became clear that the captains of these two ships were more interested in privateering than reaching Roanoke. With the coast of England still in sight, they overtook two ships and, in the words of White, "took from them whatsoever we could find worth the taking."

Their success was short-lived. Two French ships began to chase the *Brave* after it had separated from the *Roe*. The French ships were both superior to the *Brave* and had no trouble reaching it. The ships exchanged cannon fire. The *Brave*'s cannon took out its enemy's gunner, but could not stop the ship's approach. One of the French ships made contact with the *Brave*. The Frenchmen swarmed onto the English ship, and a bloody fight ensued. White reported that he was "wounded twice in the head, once with a sword, and another time with a pike, and hurt also in the side of the buttock with a shot." The fight lasted more than an hour until the Frenchmen overwhelmed the *Brave*. The English surrendered. Defenseless and without supplies, the *Brave* was forced to return to England on May 22. A few weeks later, the *Roe* also returned. Both had failed to reach Roanoke.

It wasn't until March 20, 1590, that White would set sail for Roanoke again. Two years and seven months had passed since he had left the island. White probably had mixed feelings about the voyage. Surely he was excited about the possibility of returning to his colony and being reunited with his daughter and granddaughter. At the same time, he likely feared what might have happened in the years since his departure. Because he remembered the attack gone awry at Dasemunkepeuc and the murder of George Howe, he must have been concerned that the colonists were unable to reestablish peace with the Native Americans.

White's fleet consisted of four ships, *Little John*, *Hopewell*, *John Evangelist*, and *Moonlight*. White knew from the outset that this would be a privateering mission first, and a relief mission to Roanoke second. Because of this he was not allowed to bring any colonists on this trip, nor was he able to pack anything beyond a few personal belongings. The fact that he was returning almost three years late, and without any supplies, as promised, must have further torn at his conscience.

The fleet crossed the Atlantic quickly but then spent three full months hunting Spanish ships in the Caribbean. The English overtook numerous Spanish ships, including the *Buen Jesus*, one of the finest ships in the Spanish fleet. From other ships the Englishmen stole cinnamon, wine, ginger, hides, and other commodities that could be sold for a profit back in Europe. Despite a number of English casualties, the voyage was a success. Finally, on July 30, White was able to persuade the captains of the *Hopewell* and the *Moonlight* to advance toward Roanoke.

They arrived at the harbor near Roanoke by mid-August. A column of smoke could be seen rising from the island in the distance. According to White, the smoke "put us in good hope that some of the colony were expecting my return out of England." The next morning, two boats left the anchored ships and headed to shore.

The weather worsened as the men approached Roanoke. A large wave nearly knocked over the lead boat. It managed to reach the beach, but the second boat overturned. Violent waves pounded the men as they struggled. Few could swim. They tried to hold on to the overturned boat, but the sea was too strong. Some drowned. Of the eleven men on the boat, only four survived. After the accident, the men were shaken. White managed

Artist Allen B. Doggett was also intrigued by the mysterious fate of the lost colonists and their settlement on Roanoke Island, as demonstrated by this image that dates from 1895. Throughout the centuries, many artists, writers, historians, and other scholars have tried to piece together information about what resulted with the colonists after they were left on the island by John White in 1587.

to persuade them to continue, but night had arrived, and their mission would have to wait until the next morning.

On August 18, the men reached the spot where White had left the colony. White's heart must have been pounding. His nervous anticipation probably turned to alarm when he saw no signs of the colonists. In the sand, White noticed footprints. Then, he discovered the letters *CRO* carved into a tree. White believed this was a message from the colonists. Before he had left he had instructed them to leave such a message if they ever decided to leave Roanoke. White was comforted that the message did not have a cross carved above it. A cross would have indicated that the colonists had left because they were in danger. But what exactly did the letters *CRO* mean?

As White approached the village, he discovered that the houses had been torn down and removed. The area was over-grown with weeds and grass, indicating that the colonists had left a long time ago. Carved into one of the fence posts on the out-skirts of the village, the men found the word *CROATOAN*. Like the message *CRO* found on the tree near the beach, this message did not have a cross carved above it. To White, this meant that colonists had left Roanoke for Croatoan Island, the home of their interpreter, Manteo. They had probably torn down their houses and taken them with them.

White and his crew returned to the ship anchored off Roanoke. The next morning it was agreed that they should advance to Croatoan Island. They rushed to depart, as they expected another storm. In their haste, the ship was almost run ashore. Two of their anchors got stuck in the sand. Both were cut loose, leaving them with only one. Then, the winds picked up and they were blown away from the shore before they could load their water casks. These events convinced the crew of the *Hopewell* to head for the island of Trinidad in the Caribbean to replenish their supplies instead of Croatoan. They would also be able to resume their raids on the Spanish. The plan was to return to Croatoan in the spring.

Once again, fate turned against White. Strong winds blew the *Hopewell* off course. Instead of spending the winter in the Caribbean, the *Hopewell* sailed back to England.

This is the title page from the third volume of *Principal Navigations, Voyages, and Discoveries of the English Nation*, written by English geographer and writer Richard Hakluyt. First published in 1598, Hakluyt's work details all of the progress made by the English explorers based on geographical region. Basing his writings on the direct observations of explorers, their own writings, ship logs, and other works, Hakluyt was able to reassemble the history of sea exploration from its beginnings until the sixteenth century.

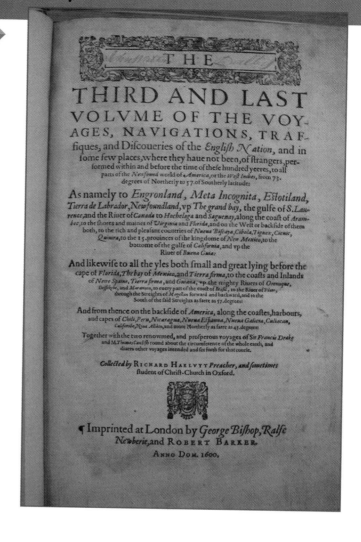

This was White's final attempt to contact the settlers. In 1593, he expressed his thoughts on the fate of the colony in a letter to Richard Hakluyt. He wrote that his colony was left to "the merciful help of the almighty, who I most humbly beseech to help and comfort them according to his most holy will and desire."

CHAPTER 6

An Unsolved Mystery

After the failed relief voyage of 1590, Sir Walter Raleigh shifted his attention away from the Roanoke colony. It wasn't until 1603 that he sponsored another voyage to Virginia. This expedition only searched the area briefly, and found no sign of the colonists.

In 1607, Jamestown was founded on the shore of Chesapeake Bay, about 120 miles (193 km) from Roanoke Island. Unlike Roanoke, this colony would survive to become the first permanent English settlement in America. Their governor, John Smith, sent several expeditions in search of the Roanoke colonists, but no traces of them were found. By 1612, Smith had given up the search.

Today, several theories have been proposed to explain what happened at Roanoke. Some historians believe that Spanish soldiers killed the colonists. Others think that they attempted to sail back to England but drowned at sea. Many more believe that Indians either killed all the colonists, or that some of them survived and were welcomed into local tribes.

Most historians believe the first theory can be ruled out. Since there is no account of such an event in any of the Spanish letters, books, or diaries that have survived the period, they believe these killings never took place.

Although the colonists might have attempted to return home, historians believe this, too, seems unlikely. White left a ship with the colonists in 1587, but none of them was experienced enough

This image of an archaeological dig on Roanoke Island was taken by a photographer working for the National Park Service in North Carolina in the 1990s. Over the years, several digs have been conducted with the help of the organization in an effort to locate remains of the 1585 and 1587 settlements, or artifacts from that period. Thus far, the most exciting discovery has been of an earthwork, or fort, which is believed to have been constructed by colonists working under Ralph Lane in 1585 or Richard Grenville in 1586. Artifacts attributed to the settlement were also found: a sickle made of wrought iron; fragments of Spanish pottery (believed to have been acquired by the colonists from Puerto Rico or Haiti on the way to America); and three metal counting devices that date from the sixteenth century and carry symbols from Tudor England.

to sail it. The colonists must have known that any attempt to reach England by boat would have likely failed, and thus avoided it.

Most historians agree that a conflict with local Indians tribes remains the most logical theory. And it is possible that some of the colonists survived and went on to live with local tribes.

This contemporary photograph shows an area where historians believe the lost colony of Roanoke possibly stood. Union soldiers stationed on Roanoke Island during the Civil War spent some of their time treasure hunting. In doing so, one of them unearthed this iron ax head in 1862. It is believed to date from the time of Sir Walter Raleigh's colony and is now part of the collection of East Carolina University. Even though various teams of archaeologists have since completed several excavations on the island, no other tools have been found. This ax head remains one of the best examples of a colonial artifact from the lost colony.

Many historians believe the colonists split into groups. If this happened, the separation may have resulted in different outcomes. For example, historians have theorized that some of the colonists went to Croatoan while others went north to Chesapeake Bay. If this occurred, then it's possible that Chesapeake Bay tribes killed some colonists, while others joined forces with Croatoan tribes.

Still, no one knows for sure what happened at Roanoke. Historians continue to search for clues in primary source documents, while archaeologists dig in the soil of Roanoke Island for artifacts. Each group believes the answers are within reach. Whether the answers can be found within a dusty book, or buried underground, they are certain the truth is out there waiting to be discovered.

June 11, 1578 — Queen Elizabeth I grants Sir Humphrey Gilbert permission to explore and settle America.

September 9, 1583 — Sir Humphrey Gilbert drowns returning from Newfoundland after an unsuccessful attempt to establish a colony there.

March 25, 1584 — Queen Elizabeth I grants Sir Walter Raleigh permission to explore and settle America.

April 27, 1584 — The scouting expedition led by Philip Amadas and Arthur Barlowe leaves England for North America.

July 4, 1584 — Scouting expedition arrives at the Outer Banks (chain of islands off the coast of present-day North Carolina).

January 6, 1585 — Sir Walter Raleigh is knighted by Queen Elizabeth.

June 22, 1585 — Ralph Lane's military colony arrives at the Outer Banks.

June 19, 1586 — Lane's colonists depart Roanoke for England on Sir Francis Drake's ships.

July 22, 25, 1587 — John White and 116 other colonists arrive at Roanoke.

August 18, 1587	— Virginia Dare becomes the first English person born in America.
August 27, 1587	— John White leaves Roanoke to return to England for supplies.
April 22, 1588	— John White departs England for Roanoke aboard the *Brave*.
May 22, 1588	— John White returns to England after an unsuccessful attempt to reach Roanoke aboard the *Brave*.
July 29, 1588	— England confronts the Spanish Armada at the Battle of Gravelines.
August 18, 1590	— White arrives at Roanoke and finds the colonists have disappeared.

PRIMARY SOURCE TRANSCRIPTIONS

Page 19: Excerpt of a transcription of Sir Walter Raleigh's *The Historie of the World*

Transcription

If fortune and chance were not sometimes the causes of good and evil in men, but an idle voice, whereby we express success, how comes it then, that so many worthy and wise men depend upon so many unworthy and empty headed fools; that riches and honor are given to external men, and without kernel: and so many learned, virtuous, and valiant men wear out their lives in poor and dejected estates?

In a word there is no other inferior, or apparent cause, beside the partiality of mans affection, but the fashioning and not fashioning of ourselves according to the nature of the time wherein we live, for whosoever is most able, and best sufficient to discern, and hath with all an honest and open heart and loving truth. If princes, or those that govern, endure no other discourse then their own flatteries, then I say such as one, whose virtue and courage forbid him to be base and a dissembler, shall evermore hang under the wheel, which kind of deserving well and receiving ill, we always falsely charge fortune with all. For whosoever shall tell any great man or magistrate, that he is not just, the general of an army, that he is not valiant, and great ladies that they are not fair, shall never be made a counselor, a captain, or a courtier. Neither is it sufficient to be wise with a wise prince, valiant with a valiant, and just with him that is just, for such a one hath no estate in his prosperity; but he must also change with the successor, if he be of contrary qualities, sail with the tide of the time, and alter form and condition, as the estate or the estates master change: Otherwise how were it possible, that the most base men, and separate from all [omitted word] qualities, could so often attain to honor and riches, but by such an observant slavish course? These men having nothing else to value themselves by, but a counterfeit kind of wondering at other men, and by making them believe that all their vices are virtues, and all their dusty actions crystalline, have yet in all ages prospered equally with the most virtuous, if not exceeded them . . .

Page 22: Title page from Thomas Harriot's *A Briefe and True Report of the New Found Land of Virginia*

Transcription

A brief and true report of the new found land of Virginia, of the commodities and of the nature and manners of the natural inhabitants: Discovered by the English

Colony there seated by Sir Richard Grenville Knight In the year 1585. Which remained under the government of twelve months, At the special charge and direction of the Honorable SIR WALTER RALEIGH Knight, lord Warden of the stannaries who therein hath been favored and authorized by her MAJESTY and her letters patents: This fore book Is made in English By Thomas Harriot; servant to the above named Sir WALTER, a member of the Colony, and there employed in discovering.

Page 27: Transcription of excerpt from Hakluyt's *Discourse of Western Planting*

Transcription

A particular discourse concerning the great necessity and manifold commodities that are like to grow to this Realm of England by the Western discoveries lately attempted, written in the year 1584 by Richard Hakluyt of Oxford at the request and direction of the right worshipful Mr. Walter Raleigh now Knight . . .

That this western discovery will be greatly for the enlargement of the gospel of Christ whereunto the Princes of the reformed religion are chiefly bound among whom her Majesty is principal.

That all other English Trades are grown beggarly or dangerous, especially in all the king of Spain his Dominions, where our men are driven to fling their Bibles and prayer books into the sea, and to forswear and renounce their religion and conscience and consequently their obedience to her Majesty.

That this western voyage will yield unto us all the commodities of Europe, Africa, and Asia, as far as we were wont to travel, and supply the wants of all our decayed trades.

That this enterprise will be for the manifold employment of numbers of idle men, and for breeding of many sufficient, and for utterance of the great quantity of the commodities of our Realm.

That this voyage will be a great bridle to the Indies of the king of Spain and a means that we may arrest at our pleasure for the space of time weeks or three months every year, one or two hundred sail of his subjects ships at the fishing in New found land.

That the riches that the Indian treasure wrought in time of Charles the late Emperor father to the Spanish king, is to be had in consideration of the Q[ueen] most excellent Majesty, least the continual communion of the like treasure from thence to his son, work the unrecoverable annoy of this Realm, whereof already we have had very dangerous experience.

What special means may bring King Phillip from his high Throne, and make him equal to the Princes his neighbors, wherewithal is showed his weakness in the west Indies.

That the limits of the king of Spain's dominions in the west Indies be nothing so large as is generally imagined and surmised, neither those parts which he hold be of any such forces as is falsely given out by the [omitted word] clergy and others his suitors, to terrify the Princes of the Religion and to abuse and blind them.

The Names of the rich towns lined along the sea coast on the north side from the [omitted word] of the main land of America under the king of Spain.

A brief declaration of the chief lands in the Bay of Mexico being under the king of Spain, with their havens and forts, and what commodities they yield.

That the Spaniards have executed most outrageous and more then Turkish cruelties in all the West Indies, whereby they are every where there, become most odious unto them, who would join with us or any other most willingly to shake of their most intolerable yoke, and have begun to do it already in [omitted word] places where they were Lords heretofore.

That the passage in this voyage is easy and short, that it cut not near the trade of any other mighty Princes, nor near their countries, that it is to be performed at all times of the year, and need but one kind of wind, that Ireland being full of good havens on the south and west sides, is the nearest part of Europe to it, which by this trade shall be in more security, and the sooner drawn to more civility.

That hereby the revenues and customs of her Majesty both outwards and inwards shall mightily be enlarged by the toll, excises, and other duties which without oppression may be raised.

That this action will be greatly for the increase, maintenance and safety of our navy, and especially of great shipping which is the strength of our Realm, and for the support of all those occupations that depend upon the same.

That speedy planting in divers fit places is most necessary upon these lucky western discoveries for fear of the danger of being prevented by other nations which have the like intentions, with the order thereof and other reasons there with all alleged.

Means to keep this enterprise from [being] overthrown and the enterprisers from shame and dishonor.

That by these Colonies the Northwest passage to Cathay [Japan] and China may easily quickly and perfectly be searched out as well by river and overland, as by sea, for proof whereof here are quoted and alleged divers rare testimonies out of the three volumes of voyages gathered by Ramses and other grave authors.

That the Queen of England title to all the west Indies, or at the least to as much as is from Florida to the Circle Arctic, is more lawful and right then the Spaniards or any other Christian Princes . . .

GLOSSARY

America Landmass consisting of the present-day continents of South America and North America.

circumnavigate To go completely around.

commodity Something useful or valued, usually meant to be sold.

conspire To secretly agree to do something.

Devonshire A county in southwestern England.

flagship The ship that carries the commander or captain of a fleet and flies the flag that identifies the fleet.

fleet A number of ships sailing together.

mariner A sailor or seaman.

palisade A fence made out of stakes, often used for military purposes.

pike A weapon made of a spearhead attached to a long pole.

pinnace A light sailing ship.

privateer A sailor or ship that is licensed to attack enemy shipping fleets. Also known as a "gentleman pirate."

shoal A sandbank or sandbar below shallow water.

sound Area of water separating the mainland from an island.

Spanish Armada Fleet of 130 Spanish warships carrying 8,000 sailors and 19,000 soldiers sent by King Philip II of Spain to attack England in 1588.

Virginia In colonial times, the territory in America claimed by Sir Walter Raleigh. It included the present-day states of Virginia and North Carolina.

FOR MORE INFORMATION

Fort Raleigh National Historic Site
1401 National Park Drive
Manteo, NC 27954
(252) 473-5772
Web site: http://www.nps.gov/fora

The Lost Colony Symphonic Drama
1409 National Park Drive
Manteo, NC 27954
(800) 488-5012
Web site: http://www.thelostcolony.org

The Museum of the Native American Resource Center
PO Box 1510
Pembroke, NC 28372-1510
(910) 521-6282
Web site: http://www.uncp.edu/nativemuseum

North Carolina Museum of History
4650 Mail Service Center
Raleigh, NC 27699-4650
(919) 715-0200
Web site: http://ncmuseumofhistory.org

Roanoke Colonies Research Office
c/o Department of English
East Carolina University
Greenville, NC 27858-4353
(919) 328-6715
Web site: http://www.ecu.edu/rcro/default.htm

Roanoke Island Festival Park
1 Festival Park
Manteo, NC 27954
(252) 475-1500
Web site: http://www.roanokeisland.com

Web Sites

Due to the changing nature of Internet links, The Rosen Publishing
Group, Inc., has developed an online list of Web sites related to the
subject of this book. This site is updated regularly. Please use this link
to access the list:

http://www.rosenlinks.com/pstc/roan

FOR FURTHER READING

Bosco, Peter I. *Roanoke: The Story of the Lost Colony*. Brookfield, CT: Millbrook, 1992.

Campbell, Elizabeth A. *The Carving on the Tree*. Boston, MA: Little, Brown, and Company, 1968.

Dolan, Edward F. *The Lost Colony of Roanoke*. New York, NY: Marshall Cavendish, 2002.

Fradin, Dennis Brindell. *The North Carolina Colony*. Chicago, IL: Children's Press, 1991.

Hilliam, Paul. *Elizabeth I: Queen of England's Golden Age*. New York, NY: Rosen, 2005.

Kent, Zachary. *The Mysterious Disappearance of Roanoke Colony in American History*. Berkeley Heights, NJ: Enslow Publishers, 2004.

Korman, Susan. *Sir Walter Raleigh: English Explorer and Author*. Philadelphia, PA: Chelsea House, 2001.

Marrin, Albert. *The Sea King: Sir Francis Drake and His Times*. New York, NY: Atheneum, 1995.

McCarthy, Shaun. *Sir Walter Raleigh*. Chicago, IL: Heinemann Library, 2002.

Rossi, Ann. *Cultures Collide: Native American and Europeans 1492–1700*. Washington, DC: National Geographic, 2004.

Staiger, Ralph C. *Thomas Harriot: Science Pioneer*. New York, NY: Clarion Books, 1998.

BIBLIOGRAPHY

Blacker, Irwin R., ed. *Hakluyt's Voyages*. New York, NY: Viking, 1965.

Conlin, Joseph R. *The American Past: A Survey of American History to 1877*. Fort Worth, TX: Harcourt Brace, 1997.

Harriot, Thomas. *A Briefe and True Report of the New Found Land of Virginia*. New York, NY: Dover, 1972.

Hulton, Paul. *America 1585: The Complete Drawings of John White*. Chapel Hill, NC: University of North Carolina Press, 1984.

Hume, Ivor Noel. *The Virginia Adventure*. New York, NY: Knopf, 1994.

Kupperman, Karen Ordahl. *Roanoke: The Abandoned Colony*. Totowa, NJ: Rowman and Allanheld, 1984.

Mancall, Peter C., ed. *Envisioning America*. Boston, MA: Bedford, 1995.

Miller, Lee. *Roanoke: Solving the Mystery of the Lost Colony*. New York, NY: Arcade, 2001.

Quinn, David B. and Alison M. Quinn, eds. *Virginia Voyages from Hakluyt*. London, UK: Oxford University Press, 1973.

Quinn, David B. *North America from Earliest Discovery to First Settlements*. New York, NY: Harper & Row, 1977.

Quinn, David B. *Set Fair for Roanoke*. Chapel Hill, NC: University of North Carolina Press, 1985.

Stick, David. *Roanoke Island: The Beginnings of English America*. Chapel Hill, NC: University of North Carolina Press, 1983.

Trevelyan, Raleigh. *Sir Walter Raleigh*. New York, NY: Holt, 2004.

Williams, Neville. *The Sea Dogs: Privateers, Plunder, and Piracy in the Elizabethan Age*. New York, NY: Macmillan, 1975.

PRIMARY SOURCE IMAGE LIST

Page 7: Hans Holbein the Younger painted this portrait of King Henry VIII in 1540 during Henry's reign. It is housed at the Palazzo Barberini at the National Gallery of Art in Rome, Italy. The adjacent sixteenth-century portrait of Queen Elizabeth, painted by an anonymous artist, is housed at the Galleria Palatina, Palazzo Pitti, in Florence, Italy.

Page 9: The sixteenth-century map of the world on this page traces Francis Drake's famous voyage around the world. It is housed at the British Library in London, England.

Page 14: John White painted this watercolor between 1570 and 1593. Like other studies of Native Americans, White was careful to observe and re-create their farming and fishing practices as accurately as possible. This image is housed at the British Museum in London, England.

Page 17: This lithograph (*Map of Raleigh's Virginia*) is a copy of a painting by John White of a map of the Virginia coastline and Chesapeake Bay. It was created sometime between 1570 and 1593.

Page 19: Simon de Passe drew this image of Sir Walter Raleigh for the title page of Raleigh's *The Historie of the World*, an account of his experiences in the New World first published in London, England, in 1614.

Page 22: This anonymous portrait (*left*) is believed to be of Thomas Harriot (also spelled Hariot) holding a spiced orange, common during Elizabethan times. It is located at Trinity College in Oxford, England. The title page of Thomas Harriot's book, *A Briefe and True Report of the New Found Land of Virginia*, is also pictured. It was first published in 1590.

Page 24: Theodor de Bry created this hand-colored engraving in 1590 based on observational drawings by John White. The de Bry engraving was then printed in Harriot's *Briefe and True Report*.

Page 27: A page from Richard Hakluyt's *Discourse of Western Planting*, a book printed in 1584 that detailed arguments for England to continually fund expeditions to colonize the New World.

Page 32: John White created this watercolor map of the eastern coastline of the United States in the 1580s.

Page 34: John White painted this image of a fish during the 1585 expedition to Roanoke.

Page 37: Theodor de Bry created this hand-colored engraving, *A Great Lord of Virginia* in 1590. It is based on a drawing done in the 1580s by John White. De Bry's engraving was printed in Thomas Harriot's *A Briefe and True Report of the New Found Land of Virginia* in 1590.

Page 42: Hendrik Cornelisz Vroom made this oil painting of a sea battle between the Spanish Armada and the English navy in 1600. It is housed at the Landes Museum Ferdinandeum in Innsbruck, Austria.

Page 47: The title page from the third volume of Richard Hakluyt's book, *Principal Navigations, Voyages, and Discoveries of the English Nation*, circa 1598. This title page is from a later edition.

Page 50: In 1862, Union soldiers unearthed this ax head, believed to be a tool used during the time of Walter Raleigh's colony. It is housed at East Carolina University.

INDEX

About the Author

Brian Belval is an editor of young adult nonfiction in New York City. His work on *The Lost Colony of Roanoke* has resulted in a continuing interest in early American history and English exploration of the New World. Recently, he has begun to research the life of Sir Francis Drake, one of England's legendary "sea dogs."

Photo Credits

Cover, p. 24 The New York Public Library/Art Resource, NY; p. 1 Library of Congress Prints and Photographs Division; p. 5 The Mariners' Museum, Newport News, VA; p. 7 (left) Palazzo Barberini, Rome, Italy/Bridgeman Art Library; p. 7 (right) Scala/Art Resource, NY; pp. 8–9 Library of Congress Rare Book and Special Collections Division; p. 13 © Guildhall Art Gallery, London, Great Britain/HIP/Art Resource, NY; pp. 14, 17, 19 Private Collection/Bridgeman Art Library; p. 18 Library of Congress, Washington D.C., USA/Bridgeman Art Library; p. 22 (left) Property of the President and Fellows of Trinity College, Oxford. Used with permission; p. 22 (right) Beinecke Rare Book and Manuscript Library, Yale University; p. 27 George A. Arents Collection, The New York Public Library, Astor, Lenox and Tilden Foundation; p. 29 © North Wind Picture Archives; p. 32 Art Resource, NY; p. 34 British Museum, London, UK/Bridgeman Art Library; p. 37 Service Historique de la Marine, Vincennes, France/Bridgeman Art Library; p. 39 © Bettmann/Corbis; p. 42 Erich Lessing / Art Resource, NY; p. 45 Picture Collection, The Branch Libraries, The New York Public Library, Astor, Lenox and Tilden Foundations; p. 47 Rare Books Division, The New York Public Library, Astor, Lenox and Tilden Foundation; p. 49 National Park Service, Fort Raleigh National Historic Site; p. 50 (top) © Raymond Gehman/ Corbis; p. 50 (bottom) Collection of East Carolina University, photo courtesy of the National Parks Service, used by permission of Charles R. Ewen, PhD.

Editor: Joann Jovinelly; **Photo Researcher:** Sherri Liberman